The Illegitimate Players present

THE GLASS MENDACITY

by Maureen Morley
& Tom Willmorth

story by Doug Armstrong
Keith Cooper
Maureen Morley
& Tom Willmorth

BROADWAY PLAY PUBLISHING INC
56 E 81st St., NY NY 10028-0202
212 772-8334 fax: 212 772-8358
http://www.BroadwayPlayPubl.com

THE GLASS MENDACITY
© 1989, 1991, 2000 by The Illegitimate Players

First printing: June 2000
I S B N: 0-88145-175-4

Book design: Marie Donovan
Word processing: Microsoft Word for Windows
Typographic controls: Xerox Ventura Publisher 2.0 P E
Typeface: Palatino
Copy editing: Michele Travis
Printed on recycled acid-free paper and bound in the U S A

The Illegitimate Players Theater Company was founded
in 1985 as a group of writers and actors dedicated to
creating original comedies for theater and television.
The company is best known for writing and producing
a series of literary parodies based on the works of
popular authors. This series was launched in 1989
with THE GLASS MENDACITY, based on three plays
by Tennessee Williams; followed by ALL MY SPITE,
based on two plays by Arthur Miller; OF GRAPES
AND NUTS, based on two novels by John Steinbeck;
and A CHRISTMAS TWIST, based on the writings of
Charles Dickens. Most plays in the series premiered
at Victory Gardens Theater in Chicago. All were taped
for broadcast by T C I of Illinois cable television.

Other plays written and produced by the company
include CHEESE LOUISE, a comedy set in the
Wisconsin Dells; PANDORA SKULNK WON'T
COME OUT OF THE HOUSE, a lighthearted look
at debilitating phobias; and MYSTERY DATE,
loosely based on the board game. Additional group
productions include three comedy revues at the Roxy
Cabaret in Chicago: NEAR NORTH SIDE STORY, OUT
ON A WHIM, and THE ILLEGITIMATE PLAYERS
COMEDY REVUE; and a twenty-four week television
series for Group W cable of Chicago.

The company won numerous awards for its theatrical,
television and cabaret productions. OF GRAPES AND
NUTS received two Joseph Jefferson Citations in
the categories of Writing/Adaption and Supporting
actress, and two "Jeff" nominations for Ensemble and

Supporting Actor. A CHRISTMAS TWIST received "Jeff" nominations for Writing/Adaptation, Ensemble, Sound Design and Costume Design. Television awards included ACE Awards for A CHRISTMAS TWIST and NEAR NORTH SIDE STORY, ACE Award nominations for THE GLASS MENDACITY and THE ILLEGITIMATE PLAYERS ON T V,and a local Emmy Award nomination for NEAR NORTH SIDE STORY.

THE GLASS MENDACITY was first presented by
The Illegitimate Players, producers Maureen FitzPatrick
and Kathy Giblin, on 22 September 1989, at the Victory
Gardens Studio Theater in Chicago, Illinois. The cast
and creative contributors were:

MITCH O'CONNOR .... Tom Willmorth
MAGGIE THE CAT .... Maureen Morley
AMANDA DUBOIS .... Maureen FitzPatrick
BRICK DUBOIS .... Himself
BLANCHE KOWALSKI .... Kathy Jensen
STANLEY KOWALSKI .... Doug Armstrong
BIG DADDY DUBOIS .... Keith Cooper
LAURA DUBOIS .... Maureen FitzPatrick

Director .... Marlene Zuccaro
Sets .... Doug Armstrong
Lighting .... Dreama J Greaves
Costumes .... Consuelo Allen
Sound design .... Jeff Tamraz
Original music .... David Whitehouse
Production stage manager .... Kathy Giblin

SYNOPSIS OF SCENES

ACT ONE

Scene One: Upstairs at Belle Reve, midday
Scene Two: Later that night

ACT TWO

Scene One: The next evening
Scene Two: The following morning

Special note on songs and recordings: For performance of such songs and recordings mentioned in this play that are in copyright, the permission of the copyright owners must be obtained. Alternatively, other songs and recordings in the public domain can be substituted.

A NOTE ON THE CHARACTERS

The characters in this play are based on original characters created by Tennessee Williams, the primary difference being that ours have a sense of humor. Some of the characters, such as Stanley Kowalski, closely reflect their source characters and require little clarification here. However, others, such as Amanda DuBois, are composites of two or more of Williams' dramatic characters and so require a closer look.

MITCH O'CONNOR is a combination of Jim O'Connor, the Gentleman Caller from THE GLASS MENAGERIE and Mitch (Harold Mitchell) from A STREETCAR NAMED DESIRE. His narrator role also links him to the character of Tom Wingfield in THE GLASS MENAGERIE, but that should not weigh heavily in the actor's portrayal. MITCH O'CONNOR, though successful, is a homebody who wants something more in life.

AMANDA DUBOIS is a combination of Big Mama from CAT ON A HOT TIN ROOF and Amanda Wingfield from THE GLASS MENAGERIE. She is flighty and flamboyant, preferring to dwell on past glories, but her devotion to her family is never far from the surface.

MAGGIE THE CAT is based on the character of the same name from CAT ON A HOT TIN ROOF. She is a scheming seductress.

BRICK DUBOIS is based on the character from CAT ON A HOT TIN ROOF. He is sullen, brooding and rendered catatonic by self-pity and alcohol; therefore, he is portrayed by a mannequin.

STANLEY KOWALSKI is based on the character from A STREETCAR NAMED DESIRE. He is similar in all respects to that character, a working-class brute, but here he is married to BLANCHE DUBOIS.

BLANCHE DUBOIS is from A STREETCAR NAMED DESIRE. A nut case. 'Nuf said.

BIG DADDY DUBOIS is based on the character of Big Daddy from CAT ON A HOT TIN ROOF. He is, as his name implies, big and bold and no-nonsense. He is father, here, to BRICK, BLANCHE and LAURA.

LAURA DUBOIS is based on the character of Laura Wingfield from THE GLASS MENAGERIE. She is painfully shy, walks with a limp, and lives in a dream world. The play was written with the assumption that LAURA and AMANDA would be played by the same actress.

A note on the play: This play, like any other, is open to a wide range of interpretation. However, it has been our experience that the script works best when played straight. As Peter Ustinov so succinctly put it, "Comedy is simply a funny way of being serious."

ACT ONE

Prologue

(MITCH *stands on the fire escape smoking a cigarette.*)

MITCH: I have no tricks in my pocket, or things up my sleeve, or wires running down my pant legs and back behind the flats where an accomplice is rigging smoke bombs. No, I'm the opposite of a stage magician. He gives you illusion that has the appearance of truth. I give you truth in the pleasant disguise of illusion. Already tonight you've seen twenty-seven fifty *(Authors' note: Feel free to substitute actual ticket price.)* disappear before your eyes, so I hope you like illusion. This play is a memory. Being a memory play, it is poorly lighted, sentimental, and decidedly non-Equity. I am the narrator of the play, and also a character in it. But I am an outsider. The rest of the characters belong to a family, who live their lives in that quaint, humid part of America called the Old South. They may seem familiar to you. There is Big Daddy and Big Amanda DuBois, and their children, Brick, Blanche, and the naive Laura. The two other characters have married into the family, but Stanley Kowalski and Maggie the Cat are as far from being kin as an ice cube is from being a shiny glass unicorn. I play a lawyer and gentleman caller, who does not appear until the final scenes. *(Pause)* Ah, what the hell, it's a memory play. I suddenly remembered that I show up in Scene One and just happen to stay the whole weekend.

As I have a poet's weakness for symbols, the DuBois represent the lost hope and broken dreams of all families everywhere. I think the rest of the play will explain itself...

Scene One

(Upstairs at Belle Reve. MAGGIE *is unpacking.* BRICK, *a mannequin, sits in a chair holding a drink.* AMANDA *flutters about them both.)*

AMANDA: My children! My children! All coming home to Belle Reve like the suckerfish in spring. It will be so lovely to see Blanche, my eldest, again.

MAGGIE: And Stanley's comin' too, isn't he, Big Amanda?

AMANDA: Oh yes, of course, Stanley too. I must tell you, Maggie, I don't know why my Blanche ever consented to marry such a beast of a man. She had so many gentleman callers as a girl. Now her sister, Laura, there's another story. Shut up in the house all the time just like a little mole. If I hadn't enrolled her in business school, she wouldn't set foot out the door. I hope you don't have troubles like I have with Laura when you eventually have a child, Maggie, as I am sure you are planning to do at any time now rather than see a poor woman laid in the ground with blood stains on her bosom from a broken heart.

MAGGIE: Big Amanda, you look so lovely today. Is that a new hairdo?

AMANDA: You like it? I copied it from a picture in a magazine. A replica of the aspic served at the reception for the Miss Palmetto contest. Of course, I wouldn't expect you to know about such things, coming from coarser beginnings.

MAGGIE: Why, I declare it's the spittin' image.
You guessed right, Brick. When we were comin' up
the walk today, the moment Brick laid eyes on you he
whispered, "Big Mama's head looks just like a big ole
aspic."

AMANDA: No! My boy Brick was always as sharp as
a grasshopper tooth, and as handsome. And such a
happy boy too. Although he's never seemed quite so
gay since he married you. You puttin' on some weight,
Maggie?

MAGGIE: I don't think so, Big Amanda. But I'd be happy
to get on a meat scale for you if it would settle your
mind.

AMANDA: I thought maybe those extra inches around
your waistline meant you and Brick finally had a little
announcement for us, Maggie.

MAGGIE: Oh, but it's Big Daddy's big day, Big Amanda.
Big Daddy comes home from the hospital today and
I just know he has a big announcement for us and it's
gonna be good news...he's gonna tell us he doesn't have
cancer.

AMANDA: Do you really think so, Maggie?

MAGGIE: I feel it like I feel my own perspiration. And
tomorrow Big Daddy's birthday will be a real party.

AMANDA: Oh, wouldn't that be wonderful, Brick?
Brick, your mama is asking you a question.

MAGGIE: He can't answer you, Big Amanda. He was
down at the high school at three in the morning last
night trying to be the big debate team hero he used to
be, and he debated himself hoarse. Isn't that right, baby?

AMANDA: Was he drunk?

MAGGIE: I reckon you'd have to be two leaves shy of
the julep to do something like that sober.

AMANDA: When a man drinks, there's trouble at home. And trouble at home starts right there. *(Points to the bed)*

MAGGIE: The light socket?

(STANLEY and BLANCHE are heard arguing outside.)

STANLEY: *(Off)* Get over here, Blanche!

BLANCHE: *(Off)* Get away from me, you big gorilla!

AMANDA: Oh, there's Stanley and Blanche. Happy voices fill the house. Let's see, I'll have them put their things in there, *(Points to side area)* and you and Brick can sleep in here. I hung a curtain up this morning so y'all will have some privacy. It's just like the pajama parties Blanche used to attend at the firehouse.

STANLEY: *(Off)* You loony old crow!

AMANDA: It reminds me of that one Sunday when I was a girl. I had seventeen gentlemen callers. We had to bring in extra folding chairs so they could all sit down, and some port-a-potties. We talked through the day, and when the sun went down we went out and searched the garden for night crawlers. The gentleman caller with the longest night crawler got to take me to the cotillion. Oh how the summer breeze carries longings of girlhood fancies.

(STANLEY and BLANCHE continue arguing.)

BLANCHE: *(Off)* Don't you come near me!

STANLEY: *(Off)* Blanche!

AMANDA: Oh, what kind of hostess am I? I must go receive my callers. *(She exits.)*

MAGGIE: Brick, I swear if that crazy woman babbled on just one more second I was about to explode. If I didn't have you here with me, I just don't know what I'd do. Did you hear that talk about havin' babies? I'm telling you, sugar, it's time. That would seal us in Big Daddy's will. You're Big Daddy's favorite, and if we can offer him a grandson, an heir, we're a sure bet to get Belle Reve when Big Daddy kicks. Oh, don't look at me like that. We all know Big Daddy's dyin'. You can smell it on him like his own sweat. I'm genuinely fond of the old coot, but we've got to face facts.

(BLANCHE *enters. Obviously confused*)

BLANCHE: *(Muttering)*...A gentleman doesn't dare talk to a southern woman in that manner. No, no, no! He must speak with love like Keats and Mr. Tennyson. This is my room. I know this room. It's a room and it was mine once. I had tea parties here with the dormouse and Carol Lawrence...

MAGGIE: Blanche, how good to see you. Did you have a pleasant trip from New Orleans?

BLANCHE: It was awful, just awful. They told me to take a streetcar named Desire, then transfer to one called Wanton Lust and then ride six blocks until I got to Gyrating Torso, but I missed the streetcar, and I had to go five miles on a bus called the number seven Bleeding Ulcer and the rest of the way on a horse with no name and I forgot that my husband Stanley was supposed to drive me and he pulled up right when I arrived. I am just perspiring like a foot. I'm going to run myself a nice hot refreshing bath with mint leaves. *(She exits to the bathroom.)*

MAGGIE: *(To* BRICK*)* They ought to change the name of this place to Belle-Vue. You and I are the only two normal people in the whole flea-bitten family. We're the only ones who could have a baby that would stand half a chance in the outside world.

(STANLEY *has entered during this line and stands in the doorway with the luggage.)*

STANLEY: If he were standin' in a department store window maybe.

MAGGIE: Mr Kowalski, it is not good manners to sneak up on people during a private conversation.

STANLEY: It ain't good manners to do it in the back seat of a Chevy neither but it's a hell of a good time. And let me tell you something. The Kowalski family has produced numerous generations of babies and most of 'em had hardly nothin' wrong with 'em at all.

MAGGIE: I have no doubt that your family breeds like locusts, Mr Kowalski, and the bowling alleys and pool halls of this great land thank you for it, but I'm talking about a child who will grow up and go to work without having to wear something metal on top of his head.

STANLEY: You think I'm common? You're right. I'm common as dirt. But you used to be common too. You married money, sweetheart, just like I did. And you prance around here in your fancy J C Penney slip with your Mr Kowalski this and your Mr Kowalski that, but underneath you're just like me...

MAGGIE: I think you need a few lessons in anatomy, Mr...

STANLEY: And I know what this poodle show is all about. You think by puttin' on airs and havin' a baby you can charm Big Daddy into leaving you the house in his will. Well, the joke's on you, sweetheart. It is common knowledge in the family that ironman over there don't shoot nothin' but blanks.

MAGGIE: How dare you fling about such vile accusations! Don't get up, Brick, I'll handle this.

STANLEY: Yeah, don't get up, Brick. Besides, you're forgettin' that Blanche is the oldest, the rightful heir, and it so happens that I have a lawyer acquaintance on his way over here...

MAGGIE: How would you ever come to have a lawyer as a friend?

STANLEY: I met him in the can at the hospital. Are you familiarized with the Napoleonic Code?

MAGGIE: If it has something to do with the can I don't care to know about it.

STANLEY: It's a law in Louisiana sayin' what goes to the goose goes to the dander. Meaning I get half of anything Blanche inherits. So I just happened to decide that it's time for Blanche and me to have a baby.

MAGGIE: Blanche have a baby? Blanche isn't capable of having a coherent thought.

STANLEY: It don't take much thought to make a baby.

MAGGIE: It does when one of the parties is locked away in a mental institution.

STANLEY: What are you gettin' at?

MAGGIE: Well, you have forced me to play my trump card, Mr Kowalski. I have in my possession papers signed by a reputable psychiatrist that certify your wife Blanche legally insane. That means I as a concerned family member can toss her onto the ice cream truck at any time. I doubt that will make either of you a frontrunner in Big Daddy's Homeowner of the Year contest.

STANLEY: You're bluffing.

MAGGIE: It happened that summer Blanche and I attended the poetry festival in Yazoo City, Mississippi. A young poet was reciting a sonnet about pigs and just as he reached the heroic couplet a stray bullet from the turkey shoot shattered the window and ended his life. Suddenly, Blanche went crazy—crazier—she tried to run out but tripped over a cord and started an electrical fire, and with the paper lanterns over all the lights, the place burned like an Irishman. When the fireman arrived on the scene, Blanche was toasting a marshmallow in the flames and singing "Where is Thumbkin?" Because Big Daddy had donated a wing to the hospital, they agreed to release her into my care. It had slipped my mind until now.

STANLEY: What does that prove? Everyone in this family is cuckoo. You said so yourself.

MAGGIE: Yes, but only your wife has the papers to prove it. Blanche is a pedigree nut.

STANLEY: Quiet, she'll hear you.

MAGGIE: Oh, she's on the other side of a curtain, she can't hear a thing.

STANLEY: (*Approaches her in a smiling, menacing way*) I want those papers.

MAGGIE: Over my dead body.

STANLEY: Give me the papers, Maggie.

MAGGIE: Brick, don't just sit there. Help me.

STANLEY: I guess I'll just have to make you give them to me. (*Lunges after* MAGGIE *and grabs her.*)

(AMANDA *enters.*)

AMANDA: Stanley, what on earth are you doing?

(STANLEY *stammers, taken aback*) Giving your brother-in-law's barren wife a hello hug before your own mama-in-law gets even so much as a kiss on the hand.

STANLEY: I'm sorry, Big Mama Amanda.

(*Hugs her. She holds out her hand. He reluctantly kisses it.*)

AMANDA: Oh Stanley, how you go on! Maggie, will you excuse us for a moment?

MAGGIE: I'd be delighted. (*exits*)

AMANDA: Stanley. Do you remember how I asked you to find a nice gentleman caller for Laura?

STANLEY: Yeah, well, I really...

AMANDA: I hope you found her someone nice. Big Daddy would be so pleased to know that Laura had a gentleman to look after her.

STANLEY: Big Daddy?

AMANDA: I had so many gentleman callers when I was a girl. Big Daddy wasn't one of them, of course, I met him through a personals ad, but I remember one Sunday I had twenty-eight gentleman callers, and we had to bring in extra folding chairs, and the police had to set up roadblocks....

STANLEY: Yeah, I brought an acquaintance of mine to meet...uh Laura. He's drivin' Big Daddy home from the hospital.

AMANDA: Oh, my word, a gentleman caller after all these years. What's his name?

STANLEY: Mitch.

AMANDA: Mitch. Sounds a little like poetry doesn't it? I knew a Mitch once, an odd boy in Brick's class. And what sort of man is this Mitch? Is he a brute like yourself?

STANLEY: No, he's a lawyer acquaintance.

AMANDA: A lawyer! Well, won't Laura be surprised?

STANLEY: I don't see why Laura can't get a date for herself. Can't she go to a bar or somethin'?

AMANDA: Oh no. Laura is a lady. It wouldn't be proper. And just between you and me, Laura is a little bit shy. She just sits by her record player playing old 45s of pop hits from the early 70s.

STANLEY: Seventies? She is screwed up.

AMANDA: And then there's her glass collection.

STANLEY: I never knew she had a glass collection.

AMANDA: Glass animals. I'll show you.

(During the next line they walk over to the cooler and AMANDA *removes the lid and takes out an animal.)*

AMANDA: Of course, she was always accidentally cutting her wrists on the unicorn so now we make her animals out of a party ice cube mold and tell her that they're glass. This one is a fox, I think, or a mountain goat. They all start to look alike after she's had them for a while. *(Tosses animal back in cooler)* Do you think your Mitch will take a fancy to our little Laura, perhaps take her dancing?

STANLEY: Big Amanda, Laura limps like a longshoreman. She ain't gonna be doin' no dancin'.

AMANDA: She has a slight pause in her step that's all. A lady must be cautious.

(BLANCHE bursts through curtain.)

BLANCHE: I feel fresh enough to take on the Vienna Boys Choir!

AMANDA: Blanche, what's gotten into you?

STANLEY: She means take them on in song, Big Mama-in-law woman. Blanche loves to sing, don't you, Blanche?

BLANCHE: Oh yes! How did that one go, the one the crawdad fisherman taught me...

AMANDA: Blanche always had the most beautiful singing voice in the Sunday choir.

BLANCHE: I remember now! "The barmaid's good, but the milkmaid's better, a bucket of cream and a wheel of cheddar, a jug of milk and a dozen eggs, spread her butter then spread her..."

STANLEY: Hadn't you better freshen up, Blanche?
You got some sweat blotches on your face.

AMANDA: Now, Stanley-man, a lady does not sweat.
Horses sweat, men perspire and ladies glow.

STANLEY: Forgive me, Big Amanda mama woman.
Blanche, you is glowing like Chernobyl after dark.
Go towel down.

(MAGGIE *enters.*)

MAGGIE: Big Daddy's come home!

(*Big commotion as they all rush to the door.* MITCH *appears in the doorway.*)

BLANCHE: Oh Big Daddy. You lost so much weight in
the hospital.

STANLEY: Stuff a sock in it, Blanche. That ain't Big
Daddy. This is my good friend, uhh...

MITCH: Mitch O'Connor.

AMANDA: Where's Big Daddy?

MITCH: Oh, he stopped to beat the field hands.

AMANDA: Well, he must be feelin' perkier. Tell us,
Mitch, is Big Daddy going to be O K?

BIG DADDY: (*Off*) The farmhands are sleepin' on the job,
and my family's all hidin' upstairs.

MITCH: I think Big Daddy would prefer to tell you
himself.

(BIG DADDY *enters.*)

BIG DADDY: Is this what you call a welcome home?

BLANCHE: Big Daddy!

(*They all rush to greet* BIG DADDY.)

BIG DADDY: Get the hell away from me, you buzzards.
I gotta lot of living left in me.

AMANDA: Does this mean you don't have cancer?

BIG DADDY: That's right, you simpering old fool.

MITCH: All Big Daddy's got is a spastic colon.

(AMANDA *is overjoyed at the news. The others respond lackadaisically.*)

BIG DADDY: Who the hell are you?

MITCH: I'm Mitch, your lawyer. I brought you home from the hospital.

BIG DADDY: That's right. You drive like a woman.

AMANDA: Praise the Lord, a spastic colon. I guess it's safe to go bake the birthday cake now. (*Exits*)

MAGGIE: That is just the most sublime news, Big Daddy. Brick and I are so happy for you we could bust.

BIG DADDY: Brick looks like he's so happy he could pass out.

MAGGIE: He had a hard time sleepin' last night.

BIG DADDY: You don't have to apologize for Brick, Maggie. A man who don't drink ain't no man.

STANLEY: I put away a case of brew a day.

BIG DADDY: A man who drinks beer spends more money on pretzels than he does on women.

BLANCHE: Stanley has bought me a trunk full of the most beautiful frocks, Big Daddy.

BIG DADDY: Then why are you wearing the dish towel you got on, Blanche?

BLANCHE: I'm saving my fine clothes for a special occasion.

BIG DADDY: What, did your bowling team make the finals, Stanley?

BLANCHE: For your party, Big Daddy! Your gala birthday party. I'll wear my fanciest ballroom gown and we'll share a waltz at dawn.

BIG DADDY: You sweat like a plowhorse when you waltz. Is that a new slip, Maggie?

MAGGIE: Why yes, Big Daddy, it is. Do you like it?

BIG DADDY: Mighty attractive. I like it better than the one you wore to visit me in the hospital.

MAGGIE: Well, a woman must respect the boundaries of propriety. But I felt so out of place...like..like an animal of some sort all pent up in a humid, sterile metallic environment...like a lion on a toaster...no...

STANLEY: So the doctor said you ain't gonna croak, huh Big Daddy-in-law?

MAGGIE: *(Muttering)* ...like a panther in a microwave. No...

BIG DADDY: Later, later. As long as Blanche is out of the damn bathroom for a minute, if y'all will excuse me... *(Exits to bathroom)*

MAGGIE: ...like a gerbil on a hibachi...

MITCH: I'm glad Big Daddy stepped out. I got some bad news.

STANLEY: You better close the curtain.

MITCH: Oh right. *(Closes curtain)* Big Daddy is dying.

MAGGIE: I thought you said he didn't have cancer.

MITCH: He doesn't. He's dying of a spastic colon.

BLANCHE: Big Daddy's dyin' of a spastic colon?

MITCH: A big spastic colon.

STANLEY: How long before he drops?

MITCH: Could be a year from now, could be tomorrow.

MAGGIE: You expect my husband and me to hang around this nuthouse for a year? Can't you be more specific?

MITCH: I'm afraid not, I'm a lawyer. But he looks pretty bad, don't you think?

BLANCHE: How do I look?

MITCH: Huh? Oh, ma'am, you...you look like the first robin of spring perched on the back fence.

BLANCHE: Please, sir, you're making me blush. Spring was such a very long time ago. Summer is long upon me. Soon it will be Labor Day and the back to school sales will commence....

STANLEY: Can it, Blanche. Mitch, did you talk to Big Daddy about the house?

MITCH: Yes. He hasn't made up his mind about who he wants to leave it to.

STANLEY: Hasn't made up his mind? This ain't the IHOP for Chrissakes. He ain't choosin' between the francheesie and the french dip.

BLANCHE: I come from a long line of French nobility.

MITCH: He's talking about a sandwich.

BLANCHE: My great granddaddy was the Earl of Sandwich.

STANLEY: Shut up, Blanche.

MITCH: I think she's charming.

MAGGIE: Blanche charming? You two must be in cahoots to swindle Brick out of his inheritance.

MITCH: *(To* STANLEY*)* Is something the matter with her?

MAGGIE: *(Screaming)* How dare you speak to me like that! Brick, do something!

STANLEY: Oh, calm down, Maggie.

MAGGIE: I can't calm down. I feel trapped just like a cat on a hot tin roof...no...

BLANCHE: That reminds me of a poem I heard once. I knew a young chippy who lived on a roof. She was thin as a shingle...

MITCH & BLANCHE: ...but never aloof.

STANLEY: Shut up, Blanche!

MITCH: Don't you tell her to shut up!

(STANLEY *retaliates and everyone is screaming and at each other's throats.* BIG DADDY *enters.*)

BIG DADDY: Look at you all, screaming, half-naked and dripping with sweat. It's good to be home.

Scene Two

(BIG DADDY, STANLEY, MITCH *and* BRICK *are at a card table playing poker.* AMANDA *sits behind the curtained area away from the game.*)

STANLEY: *(Yelling off)* Come on, Blanche, hurry up with my beer!

(MAGGIE *enters, wearing a different slip. She stands behind* BRICK.)

MAGGIE: Brother-in-law-man, why don't you run down to the kitchen and get it yourself?

STANLEY: Because I'm the man of the family, and I wear the trousers, and I'm playing cards. And when a trouser wearing man is playing cards, the wife gets the beer! Let's go, let's go, somebody bet already!

BIG DADDY: It's twenty-five to you, Stanley.

STANLEY: I know. Maybe I'm bluffing like I'm confused 'cause I'm using strategy. Let's go another fifty, you stupid sucks! *(Yells off)* Blanche, where's my beer?!

BIG DADDY: When I was your age, son-in-law-person, my whiskey was at my elbow before I knew I was thirsty. To my mind a man ain't a man if his wife ain't obedient.

STANLEY: *(Yelling off, more urgent)* Blanche!

MAGGIE: You can't be more right, Big Daddy. And if a man can't rule his own roost, how can he be put in charge of the whole coop?

BIG DADDY: You having troubles being a husband, boy?

STANLEY: No sir. *(Yelling off)* Blanche!!

MAGGIE: Maybe some men are too chicken to rule the roost.

MITCH: Actually, ornithologically speaking, a roost is ruled by a chicken.

MAGGIE: *(To STANLEY)* But if the chicken was confronted by a cat, the cat would win every time.

STANLEY: Unless the cat couldn't fight because it turned out she was fixed.

MAGGIE: Why then she'd just end up being a house cat, wouldn't she?

STANLEY: Unless she choked on a chicken bone and died.

MAGGIE: From where I stand I see only boneless chicken!

STANLEY: *(Standing)* I got your chicken bone right here, lady!

BIG DADDY: *(Standing)* Silence!

MITCH: *(Standing)* Stanley, stop!

(BLANCHE *enters. She is carrying an armload of beer bottles.*)

BLANCHE: Do not rise from your seats, gentlemen,
I cannot stay.

(They sit.)

BLANCHE: Here is your beverage, Mr Kowalski.
(She gives him a beer with an umbrella in it.) I am afraid
I may have overdone the creme de menthe.

MAGGIE: Putting mint in Stanley's beer, sister-woman?
Why that's the craziest—

STANLEY: What's crazy?! I requested it this way. Thanks
Blanche. *(Tastes beer)* Ahh! Now that's good beer.

BLANCHE: I hope it is refreshing. It is so hot! *(Fans herself
with* STANLEY's *cards)* I simply cannot take this heat.
Oh, Brother Brick, I do like the king motif on your fan.

BIG DADDY, STANLEY, MITCH: Misdeal! *(They toss in their
cards and retrieve their chips.)*

MAGGIE: Blanche! You stupid, cheating, no-neck
monster! *(She lunges at* BLANCHE's *throat, choking her.)*

BIG DADDY: You women, stop! You'll spill the drinks!

STANLEY: *(Pulling the women apart)* Knock it off! Knock it
off!

BLANCHE: I see spots. Spots before my eyes!

STANLEY: Quiet down, Blanche!

BLANCHE: *(Overdramatically lashing out at the air before
her)* Out, out damn spot! Will not all of Neptune's
oceans wash me clean?

MAGGIE: She's mad!

STANLEY: Quiet, Blanche! You hear me?! *(He slaps her
across the face.)*

MITCH: Stop it, Stanley! All of you, stop it!

(Pause. A slow, sad saxophone begins to play.)

AMANDA: Blanche, honey, come in here and keep your mother company.

BLANCHE: Very well. Mr O'Connor, I must retire to the parlor to see to the matron. Let me cool these drinks for you gentlemen. *(She puts the remaining beers into* LAURA'*s cooler.)* Adieu.

STANLEY: Hey, Mitch, you got a problem with the way I handle my wife?

MITCH: No. No, really...You... You used an open fist.

BIG DADDY: Let's gamble. Everyone sit down.

(They do.)

BIG DADDY: Hand me the deck.

(They do.)

BIG DADDY: Ante up.

(They do.)

BIG DADDY: Spit on your neighbor.

(They do.)

BIG DADDY: No, you fools! That's the name of the game!

(Lights down on poker game, lights up on AMANDA *and* BLANCHE*)*

AMANDA: Pay them no heed, Blanche. It's just the cards talking.

BLANCHE: They're mad with drink! Mr Kowalski is like something out of an Edgar Allan Poe story. Haunting and dark and evil. "Quoth the raven, 'Let's go bowling.'"

AMANDA: Perhaps before you married Stanley you should have called your mother for some courting tips.

Did you know that once I entertained thirty-five
gentlemen callers? Thirty-five!

BLANCHE: Once when I was at teacher's college, a
young merchant sailor wrote me an ode called "Hey
Blanche" and sang it to me upon an autoharp. It was
beautiful...and yet I spurned him! In heartbreak, the
sailor chained himself to his autoharp and plunged into
the raging sea.

AMANDA: He died?

BLANCHE: In anguish.

AMANDA: Of course, thirty-five is only the number of
callers who could fit into the parlor. Some two or three
hundred gentlemen callers were given bleacher seating.

BLANCHE: Alas, the dead sailor had a brother who also
sought my affections—

AMANDA: —And that doesn't include the color guard
and drill squad.

BLANCHE: He penned a ballad in praise of my legs,
which he compared to the Cliffs of Dover...and yet I
spurned him! He leapt to his death from my classroom
window, impaling himself on a tetherball pole.

AMANDA: My father had to wire the parlor into a public
address system so that I could entertain my many
wooers.

BLANCHE: Alas, as fate would have it, the dead brothers
had a cousin who was also a poet—

AMANDA: Charles Lindbergh used to write me letters.

BLANCHE: There he stood in the teacher's lounge,
an explosive device strapped to his chest....

(*Lights down on* BLANCHE *and* AMANDA, *lights up on
poker game*)

BIG DADDY: Maggie, fix me another whiskey.

MAGGIE: But, Big Daddy, you just got out of the hospital. Maybe you ought to—

BIG DADDY: Poppycock and bull! I'm stronger than Texas chili. Those doctors found nothing inside me but stubbornness. Stubbornness and a will to live! Ain't that right...uh...

MITCH: Mitch.

BIG DADDY: Mitch.

MITCH: That's right, Big Daddy. And according to the medical reports they also found twenty cents in change, a set of house keys, a lit cigarette and a pocket watch.

MAGGIE: You been taking bar bets, Big Daddy?

BIG DADDY: Nothing of the kind. I swallowed down everything in my pockets when I was in the ambulance. Wasn't about to trust my valuables to those thieving doctors. Especially a family heirloom like this. (*He pulls out a pocket watch and chain.*) Your Big Daddy got this watch from Big, Big Daddy when he died. He got it from Bigger Daddy, who in turn got it from Huge Daddy during the Confederacy. Gargantuan Daddy brought this watch with him from England three hundred years ago, and it goes to the favored child of each generation until they die.

STANLEY: Good. Who gets it now?

(MAGGIE *and* MITCH *cough.*)

MITCH: Now...that...you have all the time in the world to bequeath it yourself, sir.

BIG DADDY: I swallowed this watch to keep it safe for Brick. Ain't it something Maggie? (*He holds it out for* MAGGIE.)

MAGGIE: Oh, I don't think I should touch something that's been through your whole...family tree and all. But

I know Brick would love to have anything that you might bestow.

BIG DADDY: Not yet! I'm still living and not passing on anything. Except these two cards. Have we all bet?

STANLEY: Wait a second. Are you saying Brick is the automatic favorite or something? What about Blanche? You keep forgetting Blanche! She's the oldest. Don't that mean anything?

BIG DADDY: *(To* MITCH*)* Son, pass those pretzels over here.

STANLEY: Hey, Big Daddy, we're talking about Blanche now!

BIG DADDY: No, how 'bout those cheese balls.

STANLEY: *(Throws cheese balls at* BIG DADDY*)* Here! Now tell me about Blanche!

BIG DADDY: I'll tell you what's wrong with Blanche. She's bad luck. All her life men have been falling for her, and each one of them ends up dying. When she was growing up here at Belle Reve she was quite the flower. I lost eight good working men to Blanche. Seven were killed directly as a result of her love; the other fell into a thrashing machine while trying to learn the autoharp. A man who works the land believes in luck, and Blanche is bad luck.

STANLEY: I love Blanche and I'm not dead.

MITCH: How do we know that?

STANLEY: How do you know I'm not dead?

MITCH: No. How do we know you love Blanche?

STANLEY: How do we know I don't? How do we know anything? How do we know Big Daddy ain't going to die? *(Trying to cover his blunder)* Or you? Or me? How do we know Brick isn't already dead?

MAGGIE: (*Rubbing* BRICK's *shoulders,* BRICK *appears to try to get up, but* MAGGIE *pushes him back down*) Stay put, Brick. I won't have you get upset by this stupid, no-shirt monster.

STANLEY: Awww! I gotta take a leak. (*He starts toward bathroom.*)

BIG DADDY: Stanley! (*Stops him, then adds calmly*) You're right. How can we be certain about anything. After my scare, I intend to reevaluate the whole situation, looking at each of you children with a new keen eye. I like your guts, boy. Go pee.

(*Lights down on poker game, lights up on* AMANDA *and* BLANCHE)

AMANDA: ...so naturally I said no. What would I do as Princess of Monaco?

BLANCHE: When I was in Baton Rouge two summers ago, Napoleon Bonaparte took me out for a root beer float —

STANLEY: (*Overhearing them on his way to the bathroom*) Shut up, Blanche. Big Daddy hears you talk like that and we're through!

BLANCHE: Oh, Stanley, I didn't see you. Don't be angry. This was before we met, and Mr Bonaparte was a perfect gentleman. He kept his hand to himself.

STANLEY: You're nuts! Both you birds are nuts! Blanche, get me a beer without any mixer. Have it at my elbow when I'm done in the crapper. (*Exits into bathroom*)

(*Lights down on* BLANCHE *and* AMANDA, *lights up on poker game*)

BIG DADDY: (*Laying down his hand*) Three ladies! Beat that, Mitch.

MITCH: (*Laying down his cards*) Tally-ho! He he he he, read 'em and weep, folks.

(BIG DADDY *and* MAGGIE *look at each other and slowly shake their heads.*)

MITCH: No? Read 'em and feel guilty?

BIG DADDY: I keep telling ya, boy, there ain't no such thing as a small straight!

BLANCHE: *(Enters from behind curtain)* Don't rise. I'm just passing through to get Stanley a drink. Would Mr O'Connor like one, as I am already inconvenienced?

MITCH: I would be pleased, Ms Blanche.

MAGGIE: Her name is Kowalski. Mrs Kowalski. Don't forget that.

BLANCHE: *(With beer for* MITCH*)* Here you are. Why, it's hotter than thighs on a car hood! Are you the dealer, Mr O'Connor?

MITCH: I think so. *(To* MAGGIE*)* How many points is that worth?

MAGGIE: Our Mr O'Connor is not overly familiar with the game.

BIG DADDY: Shame and tarnation! A man that don't know poker is a man that don't know squat!

MITCH: I do too know squat, Big Daddy!

BLANCHE: I know him too. I was courted by Mr Squat as a girl. *(Beginning to leave)* The fair Mr Squat of the Nashville Squats....

MITCH: Ms Blanche, would you like to pick the game?

MAGGIE: How about Crazy Eights?

BLANCHE: I've always been fond of Wild Queens.

MITCH: Wild Queens it is!

BIG DADDY: Stanley, boy! If you want to play get yourself out here!

STANLEY: *(Enters)* I'm here. What's the game, Mitch?

MITCH: Do you know Wild Queens?

STANLEY: No, but I bet ya Brick here knows a couple.

BIG DADDY: What's that you say about my son?!

MAGGIE: You're drunk, you filthy monster!

MITCH: You mean Brick is —

BIG DADDY: Lies and Mendacity!

MAGGIE: Everyone here knows that Brick is a real man! He was captain of the wrestling team in high school.

BIG DADDY: Wrestle him Brick! Right here!

(BRICK *begins to rise out of his seat again, but* MAGGIE *stops him.)*

MAGGIE: No, he will not! You savage men and your savage ways. Any time your manhood is questioned you leap to the floor and grapple! I can tell you for a fact that Brick is one hell of a man.

STANLEY: Enough to make a grandson, Maggie?

MAGGIE: OK, so he's one heck of a guy. But he's also got all your money, you ape-based creature!

MITCH: Anthropologically speaking, we're all ape-based creatures. Some, like Stanley, just haven't lost the hair on their backs.

BIG DADDY: Am I playing poker with Charles Darwin?! Now stop! Tomorrow is my birthday, and I want to play poker til the sun comes up! Amanda, you gonna have a birthday cake for your man?

AMANDA: Oh, yes! A big cake, with lots of candles, and "Congratulations Big Daddy You Don't Have Cancer" written on it in blue icing! *(Shows him birthday cards)* And just look at all the birthday cards you received. I can recall the times on Blue Mountain when—

BIG DADDY: Shut you up! And I want dancing...lots of dancing on the front lawn, and music by some Hispanic people in poofy pants, and lots of...aghh!... *(He clutches his stomach.)*

MAGGIE: Big Daddy!

AMANDA: Big Daddy, are you feeling poorly?

BIG DADDY: Git off me, you women! It's only my spastic colon!

AMANDA: Let me fix you a Maalox julep.

BIG DADDY: Do you hear me, woman! I'm fine! It was the thought of one of your lead cakes that doubled me over.

(STANLEY, MAGGIE, MITCH and BRICK are staring at BIG DADDY.)

BIG DADDY: Why do my children stare at me so?

(BRICK looks away.)

BIG DADDY: We all know that I am going to live! *(After a slightly significant pause, all nod overanxiously.)* Ask Rich, he was at the hospital.

MITCH: I... You're as fit as a man in your condition has a right to be, Big Daddy.

BIG DADDY: Let's play poker. Big Amanda, go through those cards and see if I got any gift money. I feel a roll coming on. *(To MITCH)* Your deal, boy.

MITCH:	AMANDA:
Here we go....one, one, one, one, two, two, two, two, three, three, three, three, four, four, four,—	What is this? A letter from Laura's business college. Maybe it's her graduation announcement. *(Opens it)* Oh my lord! This cannot be! This just cannot be!

BLANCHE: Is Laura in trouble at school?

BIG DADDY, MAGGIE, STANLEY: Stop it!

AMANDA: *(Rushing off)* Laura! Laura!

MITCH: I'm sorry. Maybe I shouldn't play.

BIG DADDY: Nonsense, we need a fourth.

MITCH: Now, I have one quick question...

BIG DADDY, MAGGIE, STANLEY: *(Exasperated)* High card, pair, two pair, three of a kind, straight, flush, full house, four of a kind, straight flush.

MITCH: Thanks.... Wait, what was the second one?

BIG DADDY: This is poker, boy! Shit or get out of the pot!

MITCH: I'm doing both. I'm out.

(MITCH leaves the table and heads toward the curtain. After a pause, BIG DADDY, MAGGIE, and STANLEY dash to peek at his cards. MAGGIE then sits on BRICK's lap.)

(Lights down on poker game, lights up on BLANCHE and MITCH)

BLANCHE: Have you come to join me for a drink, kind sir?

MITCH: Actually, I'm looking to use the little cowboy's room. Is it utilized?

BLANCHE: No. Stanley just relinquished it.

MITCH: Ah. Perhaps I will have a drink, Miss Blanche.

BLANCHE: Splendid. What shall I call you, Mr O'Connor?

MITCH: Please call me Mitch.

BLANCHE: *(Ready to pour a drink)* Very well...Mitch. Scotch?

MITCH: No, it's Irish, I believe. Blanche is French, is it not?

BLANCHE: Yes. Blanche means "white." My last name is DuBois, which means "woods." So my full name means 'white woods.'

MITCH: It's beautiful. Of course, you are now Blanche Kowalski.

BLANCHE: What an ugly name—Kowalski! Whatever does it mean?

MITCH: It's a Polish word which, as I recall, translates roughly into "hen pantry."

BLANCHE: I prefer the imagery of a white wood better. Don't you, Mitch?

MITCH: I prefer the imagery, yes.

BLANCHE: Oh, how you look me up and down!

MITCH: I'm sorry, I....

BLANCHE: Do not apologize. It only goes to show that you have the eye of an artist. A sculptor perhaps?

MITCH: Oh, no, no.

BLANCHE: A painter?

MITCH: Well...hardly. I once tried art school, drew Stinky the Skunk very well, but I flunked the pirate, and lost the scholarship. That must sound foolish to you. A grown man failing a correspondence art course.

BLANCHE: No! Art is the most difficult of the humanities. I couldn't draw a pirate for my life. Although I tend to draw sailors for some reason.

MITCH: You are looking at a man lacking in all of the important humanities; I can't play poker, I can't bowl...I've never once attended a monster truck event. I'm not very exciting, am I?

BLANCHE: On the contrary. I find it refreshing that you are so inept at anything masculine. What do you do, Mr O'Connor? Your line of endeavor.

MITCH: I'm a lawyer.

BLANCHE: A lawyer! My, my! The many mysteries of Mitch O'Connor. May I smoke?

MITCH: Yes. Please take one of mine. (He offers his case.)

BLANCHE: What a fine cigarette case.

MITCH: Yes. This is my most prized possession. If I were ever rushed to a hospital, this is the belonging I would want to eat. Look at the inscription. You're an English teacher, perhaps you'll recognize it.

BLANCHE: The writing is so small.

MITCH: It's Hamlet.

BLANCHE: I still can't make it out. What quote is it?

MITCH: No. It's Hamlet. The entire play is engraved on the lid of this case.

BLANCHE: It must come from someone very special...with an awful lot of spare time.

MITCH: It's from my mother.

BLANCHE: Oh, you dear, sweet boy.

MITCH: This may sound crazy, Blanche, but I'm not satisfied with my life.

BLANCHE: But you are a lawyer. And a success, unlike some men that I do know.

MITCH: Yes, I'm a successful New Orleans lawyer, I make more money than most Latin American countries, I own lots of things, but so what! My life is empty, Blanche. Emptier than a Mormon wet bar. You see, well...I still live with my mother. I know that sounds funny, a man of my years being a—

BLANCHE: No! I don't think you're an aging, effeminate, boot-licking mama's-boy!

MITCH: I was going to say "stay-at-home."

BLANCHE: I think it most gallant.

MITCH: You see, my mother is sick.

BLANCHE: You mean ill, like Big Daddy?

MITCH: No. She's just a sick woman. Sick in her mind. Two bricks shy of a load. Senile. You don't reproduce a five-act Elizabethan drama with a diamond-tipped eyebrow hair and come off normal. I really should strike out on my own. I know I should. But Mother loves me. She's now doing the War of the Roses trilogy on a lighter. How can I leave her?

BLANCHE: I am touched by that. Let's put on one of Laura's records. (*She goes to the Victorola and plays "Da-Do-Run-Run" by Shaun Cassidy.*)

MITCH: I never thought I could leave her, that is, until this weekend. Until I saw you.

(BLANCHE'*s eyes start to look slightly crazed.*)

MITCH: Please hear me out. I could never love other girls. No matter how young and kind and perfect they were, they were never...well, they were never my mother! But you, Blanche, (*He grabs* BLANCHE.) You are young, beautiful, kind...and insane. I need you, Blanche.

BLANCHE: Mr Bonaparte, control yourself, please!

MITCH: I know it's crazy, and so are you, but please—

STANLEY: What's keeping you, Mitch?! Did you fall in?

MITCH: Yes, but I'm all right! (*To* BLANCHE) Blanche talk to me!

BLANCHE: Do you play the autoharp?

(*Lights come up on the full stage.*)

STANLEY: Let's cut the cards, huh? And shut off that music! It's crap!

BIG DADDY: It's mendacity. Worse, it's Shaun Cassidy!

STANLEY: *(Getting up)* Come on, Blanche, do as I tell you and turn off that—

(STANLEY *whips open the curtain, revealing* BLANCHE *and* MITCH *in an embrace.)*

STANLEY: What the hell is this, Mitch?

BLANCHE: Is it not plain, Stanley? As plain as my shame?

STANLEY: Quiet, Blanche. *(To* MITCH*)* What were you two—

BLANCHE: Mitch was making known his love for me, and forcing his passions upon me.

STANLEY: *(Whispering violently to* BLANCHE*)* I said quiet, Blanche! Don't get loopy on me now!

BLANCHE: But Mitch loves me!

MAGGIE: *(For* BIG DADDY *to hear)* Blanche, you speak like a mad woman.

BLANCHE: Mitch, *mon cheri*, explain it.

MITCH: Blanche grabbed me...she was choking on something... *(He searches)* ...on the rubber end thing that goes on a sofa leg. I gave her the Heimlich Maneuver, and you came in.

STANLEY: *(To the others)* See?

MITCH: The oxygen couldn't get to her head, I guess, causing her to appear mad to the uninformed.

STANLEY: Right. Good work, Mitch, I owe you one. In fact, can I owe you five hundred? Brick keeps raising.

MITCH: Oh, who am I kidding? Stanley, let me get this out in the open...

STANLEY: What?

AMANDA: *(Off stage)* I said get up there, Laura!

LAURA: *(Off stage)* But Mama!

AMANDA: *(Off stage)* Get up there and speak with your father, NOW! *(Slap!)*

BIG DADDY: You men, hush up. Let's take a break for a minute. Laura's coming.

MITCH: I think this should be said, Big Daddy.

BIG DADDY: Take it outside, you hear? Brick, Maggie, give way. That slap sounds like a father/daughter talk is about to commence.

MAGGIE: Come on, Brick. *(Lifts BRICK)* Oh, baby, you can hardly stand! We better get you some air. *(She drags BRICK out the door.)*

STANLEY: I need a cig. Come on Mitch, you can do your talking on the fire escape.

(STANLEY and MITCH leave.)

BLANCHE: Mr O'Connor! Am I no longer a mother to you?

BIG DADDY: Blanche, honey, why don't you run down to the corner store and get Big Daddy some pipe tobacco. *(Gives BLANCHE a poker chip)* They know the family. They take poker chips.

BLANCHE: *(Exiting)* Well, it's hippity-hop to the barber shop to buy a piece of candy!

BIG DADDY: Laura, come in here, child.

(LAURA enters to music.)

BIG DADDY: You been keeping yourself scarce, Laura. Aren't you happy to see your Big Daddy home?

LAURA: Oh, yes. I'm sorry. *(She goes and embraces* BIG DADDY.*)*

BIG DADDY: Not too tight.

LAURA: Mama wanted me to show you this. It's from my business school. *(Gives a letter to* BIG DADDY, *who reads it)* Oh, my record collection! *(Goes to the record player)* Records mustn't be left out. They'll get dusty or scratched. Oh, my Bay City Rollers!

BIG DADDY: Deception! Deception!

LAURA: I hope it's not ruined.

BIG DADDY: Laura!

LAURA: *(Timid)* You see, they no longer record... and unless they have a reunion tour—

BIG DADDY: You gonna be graduating from business school this spring, daughter-woman?

LAURA: I hope so.

BIG DADDY: Don't lie to Big Daddy!

LAURA: Is there a registrar mistake?

BIG DADDY: Hear me, girl!

LAURA: My thesis was ready—!

BIG DADDY: Mendacity!

LAURA: — but a dog ate it...!

BIG DADDY: Mendacity! Nothing but mendacity! You aren't getting a business degree this spring because you haven't been to school in four years!

LAURA: I couldn't, Big Daddy, I just couldn't! On the first day of class I arrived late and had to walk into the lecture hall after all the others had been seated. They were all looking at me, glaring, and my leg clumping along!

BIG DADDY: You don't limp.

LAURA: I do! And I had to walk all the way to the far row to find a seat. Everyone was watching, I knew they could hear my heart pounding in my sweater! Minutes dragged to hours. My leg snagged the extension cord to the overhead projector, and it followed me to my seat. Then the professor asked my name for the attendance book, and I was so nervous I vomited! The whole class was staring and heaving, and before I knew what I was doing I ran! I ran all the way home from business school and I couldn't go back! I just couldn't, Big Daddy.

BIG DADDY: Well, that explains your grades. It also explains the overhead projector in your closet.

LAURA: I'm sorry to have deceived you and Mama.

BIG DADDY: For four years we thought you were training your mind. What were you doing?

LAURA: Sometimes I would go to the movies or maybe the library. But my favorite place was the zoo. They have entire menageries of so many creatures.

BIG DADDY: What happened to the tuition checks I sent with you?

LAURA: Have you seen the new oceanarium?

BIG DADDY: Business school was your future! Now what?

LAURA: I'd like to go vomit.

BIG DADDY: All right. I'll join you.

(BIG DADDY *and* LAURA *exit out door. Lights come up on* STANLEY *and* MITCH *on fire escape.*)

STANLEY: The first time I did it I admit I was a little nervous. All the guys said it was impossible, you can't take 'em both at the same time. But I told 'em, you just gotta have the right touch, and damned if I didn't lay the two of 'em down that Saturday night. My first seven-ten split. And we took the tournament.

MITCH: Wow, that's really an exciting story.

STANLEY: But you didn't bring me out here to talk about bowling.

MITCH: Yes I did. I did, really.

STANLEY: Quit stalling. What did you want to talk to me about?

MITCH: Well, you remember what it was like when you first started seeing Blanche?

STANLEY: Yeah.

MITCH: Well, then maybe you'll understand how I feel.

STANLEY: I remember on hot summer nights like this one, Blanche and me used to come out on this fire escape.

MITCH: Sounds romantic.

STANLEY: And she'd give me a hickey for every moth I could catch and eat.

MITCH: Maybe you wouldn't understand.

STANLEY: Hey, Mitch, I stood next to ya in the john. You can tell me anything.

MITCH: I'm afraid.

STANLEY: Afraid? Oh, because of how I acted inside. Don't take that personally. I just saw you there with Blanche and jumped to conclusions. A man's gotta protect his wife, right? If I ever thought someone was trying to muscle in on my meal ticket, particularly now

that's it's almost time for dessert, I'd tear him limb from
limb. But you don't have to worry about that, pal...
unless you came out here to tell me you want to screw
my wife.

MITCH: Ha, ha. Of course not. Are you kidding?
Who would want to screw your wife?

STANLEY: What?

MITCH: I mean everyone wants to, but nobody would
be stupid enough to.

STANLEY: That's better. So what did you want to talk
to me about?

MITCH: Uhh...I'm participating in a walk-a-thon in a
couple of weeks, and I wonder if you'd sponsor me.

STANLEY: No problem. As long as it don't cost anything.

MITCH: Uhh...great. I'm gonna go downstairs for a
sandwich. Coming?

STANLEY: In a minute. I wanna see if any moths are out
yet.

(MITCH *exits.* MAGGIE *enters the room and pulls a slip out
of her suitcase and dabs at her face, neck and chest with it.
Meanwhile,* STANLEY *enters from the fire escape and
watches, unseen by* MAGGIE. *She pushes one strap of
the slip she's wearing off her shoulder.*)

STANLEY: I didn't know that cats shed their skin.

(MAGGIE *spins around to face him.*)

MAGGIE: You startled me. Don't you ever announce
your presence?

STANLEY: I make my presence known in many ways.

MAGGIE: Standing there watching me undress, licking
your chops. Will you kindly avert your eyes?

STANLEY: I'll avert my whole head. *(He turns around.)* But I was here first, Maggie. It was you who snuck up on me. But do not forget I am a married man.

MAGGIE: Don't make me laugh. I just came up here to change into my sleeping slip. I'm still in my poker slip, in case you hadn't noticed.

STANLEY: I noticed.

MAGGIE: *(Pulls strap back onto her shoulder)* All right. You may turn around.

STANLEY: You haven't changed. Don't you feel like sleeping anymore?

MAGGIE: I couldn't sleep a wink with you slinking around in the dark.

STANLEY: Do I make you nervous, Maggie? *(Takes a swig out of the whiskey bottle)*

MAGGIE: Of course not.

STANLEY: *(Moving toward her)* Then why are you all hot and tense and twitchy like a gnat on a warm can of soda? I know what you need. *(Moves even closer)*

MAGGIE: What?

STANLEY: You need to take off that slip and feel something different rub up against your body, something firm and strong that feels good against your skin. You need a cotton slip. *(Exits)*

END OF ACT ONE

ACT TWO

Scene One

(MITCH *once again appears on the fire escape.*)

MITCH: With the fiasco of Laura's business schooling revealed, and the lies about Big Daddy's condition eating away at the household like a termite with a thyroid disorder, it became imperative that the family go ahead with Big Daddy's birthday party. To cheer him with the gift of mendacity.

But lies are an insidious gift. Once given, you cannot take them back. You must simply hope that the transparent tissue wrapping paper of deceit is enough to keep the recipient from seeing through to the stainless-steel fondue pot of truth.

It is now the next evening, and the crisply tied bows and ribbons around the family's deceit are about to come undone.

(BLANCHE *is brushing* LAURA's *hair*)

LAURA: Ouch, Blanche! You're pulling my hair.

BLANCHE: Now Laura, you can't go downstairs to the birthday party looking like a frump. You must beautify yourself or you'll never get a man.

LAURA: No man would ever want me.

BLANCHE: You mustn't say that, sister-gimp.

LAURA: I have a limp, and I'm shy, and when I get tense I vomit.

BLANCHE: In addition, you have the beginnings of a bald spot at the top of your head.

LAURA: You see? *(She moves away)* Would you like to hear my favorite record played upon the Victorola? *(She takes out a piece of tattered cardboard)* It's a Bobby Sherman song, published on the back of a Raisin Bran box when we were girls. I still play it every day.

BLANCHE: Laura, we mustn't tarry. The party is commencing, and you will miss your gentlemen callers. Big Amanda said you might be receiving one today.

LAURA: A caller?...For me?...

BLANCHE: Of course! Don't gentlemen call here at Belle Reve anymore?

LAURA: An occasional Jehovah's Witness.

BLANCHE: No suitors? *(A pause)* Have you never once loved a man?

LAURA: In high school I had a...a crush, you might say. He was in Brick's class, older than me. He didn't know I was alive. He was the smartest boy in school and would sing and dance in all the glee club musicals. Here's the program from *The Pirates of Penzance*. He signed it for me.

BLANCHE: How gallant. What is the inscription?

LAURA: No words. Just a cartoon of a skunk.

BLANCHE: A skunk?

LAURA: You see, he played the Pirate King, but he couldn't draw pirates, he said, so he drew me this skunk.

BLANCHE: He drew...a skunk? STINKY THE SKUNK?!

LAURA: I don't know if it has a name. I have a skunk in my glass collection named "Dribbles."

BLANCHE: *(Going mad)* Let me see it! It is Stinky. It is Stinky!!

LAURA: I thought it quite good.

BLANCHE: My two-timing poet boy! Alas, the green-eyed monster jealousy, making the skunk with two backs!

LAURA: Blanche, are you unwell?

STANLEY: *(Entering)* Hey, you two, better get on downstairs. The ice cream's getting cold.

BLANCHE: *(To* LAURA*)* Mammy, rope me into my corset. *(She puts something silly about her waist.)*

STANLEY: Blanche! I said now! *(Throws* BLANCHE *toward exit)*

BLANCHE: You brute!

STANLEY: And you too, Laura.

*(*LAURA *shies away)*

STANLEY: I mean it! Go!

LAURA: Brother-man, I fear you.

STANLEY: Do as I say!

LAURA: You're yelling at me.

STANLEY: Then do as I yell!

LAURA: I am ill to my stomach! *(She rushes into the bathroom and locks the door.)*

STANLEY: Come out of there, Laura! Blanche, get her out of the john, will ya?

BLANCHE: A woman preparing for a party is not to be rushed.

STANLEY: Blanche, listen to me. You gotta get Laura downstairs and buy me some time alone. Maggie the Cat has the goods on you, a report from some head shrinker that's going to put you away for life if I don't find it!

BLANCHE: I don't recall a head shrinker. I once saw a man regarding my hips and thighs—.

STANLEY: Get downstairs!

BLANCHE: Very well. It is so hot! *(She exits.)*

STANLEY: Laura, go downstairs, sweetheart. Blanche just went.

LAURA: *(Behind door)* I'm scared.

STANLEY: I didn't mean to scare you, honey. I'd a' used an open fist. Here, let me play one of your records for you. Come out here and help me pick one, Laura. *(Silence)* Laura?

LAURA: *(Behind door)* What.

STANLEY: What do you wanna hear? Pick anything.

LAURA: *(Behind door)* "Muskrat Love."

STANLEY: Anything but that. How about... *(He searches.)* "Afternoon Delight" by Starland Vocal Band.

LAURA: *(Behind door)* The what vocal band?

STANLEY: Starland.

LAURA: *(Behind door)* What?

STANLEY: Starland! *(Slower and deliberately)* Star—land.

LAURA: *(Behind door)* What?

STANLEY: *(Drops to his knees, with pained look on face)* Who cares! Get out of the head!!

MITCH: *(Entering)* Stanley, I've looked everywhere. We need to talk.

STANLEY: Good, 'cause I need your help on something.

MITCH: It's about Blanche.

STANLEY: Exactly. It looks like she might be committed.

MITCH: I know it might look that way, Stanley, but she's not committed.

STANLEY: Not yet anyway.

MITCH: She may love you, but—

STANLEY: Listen, the problem right now is Laura.

MITCH: She wants out, Stanley.

STANLEY: Then why did she lock the door?

MITCH: I don't know. (Pause) What door?

STANLEY: To the can! Laura's locked herself in. If we're going to save Blanche, you've got to get Laura downstairs for me, just for a few minutes. Can you do that for me, Mitch?

MITCH: But how? I don't recall ever meeting Laura.

STANLEY: Who does?

MITCH: What's she like?

STANLEY: Nice girl, kinda shy, has a...slight limp.

MITCH: Oh.

STANLEY: But she knows how to use it. It's important, Mitch, or I wouldn't be asking. Just get her to go to the party with you, whatever it takes. Please.

MITCH: All right. I'll do it for Blanche.

STANLEY: Good man.

MITCH: And twenty bucks.

STANLEY: Friggin' lawyer. (Gives him money) Here! But hurry before I'm missed downstairs.

MITCH: You're covered for a while. Big Daddy mistook the cake for a pinata, so they're reupholstering the parlor.

STANLEY: Laura, honey, there's someone here for you. A gentleman caller.

LAURA: *(Behind door)* One moment.

STANLEY: *(To* MITCH*)* Whatever it takes, buddy. Whatever it takes. *(He hides.)*

(Soft music as LAURA *enters, shyly thumping toward* MITCH*)*

MITCH: Hi, my name's Mitch. You must be limping. —LAURA!

LAURA: You must be here for Big Daddy. Are you selling veteran's insurance?

MITCH: Actually, I'm here to see you.

LAURA: Me? *(She shies away.)*

MITCH: Yes. I thought you might accompany me to the birthday festivities. Big Daddy is about ready to open his gimp. —GIFTS!

LAURA: I'm giving Big Daddy one of my glass animals. Would you like to see them?

MITCH: Sure. I'd like that. Why don't have a seat here on the crutch. —COUCH!

LAURA: *(Showing animal cubes)* This one is a marmoset. And this is a spotted leopard. I feared I had lost it once, but it was only hiding in Mama's lemonade. My favorite of all is the unicorn. I wrapped it up to give to Big Daddy for his birthday.

MITCH: When did you start collecting as if I cared.

LAURA: In high school.

MITCH: High school? Wait one cotton-picking minute! I thought you looked familiar. We went to high school together. I knew Brick had a younger sister. You must be she!

LAURA: I'm afraid so.

MITCH: When I first saw you in that doorway I almost called you a name—

LAURA: Lots of people do.

MITCH: Only it wasn't a name. It was like a nickname...

LAURA: Was it..."Blue Roses?"

MITCH: Yes! We used to call you Blue Roses. Why was that?

LAURA: Well, when I was in ninth grade I had pleurosis, but everyone thought I said "blue roses," and the name stuck. In tenth grade I had gastritis, but people thought I said "class riots," and that name stuck too. Then in eleventh grade I had bronchitis, but people thought I said "brown cow tits"...that was the worst year of my life.

MITCH: Yeah, high school can be tough.

LAURA: I remember you too. You were such a good dancer. I used to sit on the side of the gym in my oxygen tent, watching you dance with your friends. You were so popular.

MITCH: That's hardly so.

LAURA: You were good in everything, and everyone liked you.

MITCH: Pshaw. You only believed what they wrote about me in *The Torch*.

(LAURA *goes to a bookshelf and picks up a yearbook.*)

MITCH: A yearbook can give you a strange perspective of a person. What's that you're—? Oh, my! *The Torch!*

LAURA: *(Reading a clipping)* "Not only is Mitchell O'Connor most likely to succeed, he's really neat and cool and funny."

MITCH: I wouldn't have come off so good if I hadn't been the editor.

LAURA: *(Turning a page)* And here you are in the school musical. When you sing it's like... Oh, I do go on!

MITCH: When did you hear me sing, Laura?

(A long pause. In echo, I Am the Pirate King *is sung in great baritone.)*

MITCH: You say you heard me sing?

LAURA: Oh, yes. In high school. I saw *The Pirates of Penzance* all three times.

MITCH: I am honored, Laura. You kept coming back to see me?

LAURA: Actually, the brace I wore on my leg got stuck in the seat at the auditorium. I stayed all weekend long. But what a weekend it was.

MITCH: You should have called for a janitor.

LAURA: I was too shy.

MITCH: Laura, you know what I judge to be the trouble with you? I mean, besides your gruesome deformity. You have an inferiority complex you could drive a truck through. Now stop! You must say to yourself, "I am Laura DuBois, and I am unique to all the world, and I can do anything I want, and if anyone tries to drive a truck through my gaping complex, I'm going to fight them tooth and nail! Now say it!

LAURA: It's so many words.

MITCH: Then listen to me, Laura. Make a wish, anything in the world, and I'll tell you how to make it come true.

LAURA: All right. In high school, when I was watching you dance with all those other girls, I used to dream that someday, ...oh, I don't know...   END

MITCH: Say, Laura, let's you and I go back in time, just for tonight. I'll take you downstairs and request a slow, romantic song...then you can watch me dance with the other women, what do you say?

LAURA: If I wouldn't be in the way.

MITCH: I'll see to it.

(MITCH and LAURA exit. Quickly, STANLEY reenters. Indistinguishable music and chatter are heard during STANLEY's time alone onstage.)

STANLEY: OK, where would I hide something if I was a broad? No, no, where in the room would I hide something if I was a broad? Under the bed. (Looks) Where? Where? (Rummages through the ice in the cooler, pops a couple ice cubes in his mouth) Suitcase. (Goes through suitcase, throwing things on the floor) Hey, this is my suitcase. (Goes through MAGGIE's suitcase, pulls out slinky black negligee) This must be for funerals. (Looks it over some more and then rushes over and splashes his face in the cooler, looks up, for a moment forgetting what he was doing) Papers! That's right. (He goes back and continues going through the suitcase. He finds the papers in an envelope, opens it, looks at papers, kisses them and shoves them back in envelope, starts to put them in his suitcase.) No. Better get rid of 'em for good. Matches.

(Starts to search himself for matches, absently throws the papers on the table. Immediately, the party bursts in with BRICK leading the conga line, followed by MAGGIE, MITCH, BLANCHE, AMANDA and BIG DADDY. They all throw

presents down on the table on top of the papers before
STANLEY *can stop them.)*

AMANDA: Since naughty ol' Stanley wouldn't come
downstairs for Big Daddy's birthday party, we brought
Big Daddy's birthday party up here to Stanley.

STANLEY: You didn't have to do that. Go on back down.
I'll be down in a minute.

BIG DADDY: Go back down nothin'! That crazy woman
done dragged me up all these stairs and I'm stayin'.
(Plops into chair next to table)

STANLEY: These presents must all be in your way,
Big Daddy. You want me to clear the table?

BIG DADDY: No, I don't. I've seen the way you clear
a table. And if any one of you bought me something
other than dimestore trash for a change, I want it in
one piece when I open it.

AMANDA: I love birthday parties. All the laughter and
gaiety.

BIG DADDY: Let's see. This one's from Big Amanda.
(Opens present) What in blazes is this?

AMANDA: Why, it's a Spirograph set, Big Husband.
I didn't know if you'd be out of the hospital, and I
thought you'd like something to keep you occupied.

BIG DADDY: Stop treating me like a child, wife-woman.
A man who ain't graduated to an Etch-A-Sketch ain't
no man.

AMANDA: I'll exchange it in the morning, when I return
all the other gifts.

BIG DADDY: That's more like it. *(Picks up another box)*
Hmmm. From Laura. I hope its not another wax
dolphin from the zoo. Where is Laura, anyway?

AMANDA: I don't know. She was on the end of the conga line when we started up the stairs. I'll go fetch her.

BIG DADDY: Leave her be. She's gotta learn to fend for herself. *(Opens box)*

BLANCHE: She was excited about her gift this year. She picked out the glass unicorn from her collection just especially for you.

BIG DADDY: *(Looks in box)* Unicorn piss. I gotta have a talk with that girl.

MAGGIE: Open this one next, Big Daddy. This is from Brick and me. Brick picked it out himself and wrote out the card.

BIG DADDY: His name's spelled wrong.

MAGGIE: Brick is such a prankster. And look how he keeps such a straight face. That's very funny, baby.

BIG DADDY: Never dot your "i"s with hearts, boy, it ain't manly.

STANLEY: But it sure is pretty, ain't it, Maggie? Pretty writin' for a pretty boy.

MAGGIE: It must be difficult for you to write, brother-man, not having an opposable thumb and all.

BIG DADDY: Enough! If I sit in this chair much longer, I'm gonna burn a hole straight through it. What's this? Oh, it's a calendar. How come it's only got six months?

MAGGIE: Oh, never mind that, Big Daddy. *(Gesturing toward table)* Look, more gifts!

BIG DADDY: *(Grabs another package)* This one's from Mitch. Who the hell is Mitch?

MITCH: I am, Mr Big Daddy.

BIG DADDY: Oh yeah, the lawyer fella. What are ya up to, there?

MITCH: Taking inventory of the estate...er...gifts.

BIG DADDY: What in tarnation for?

MITCH: Uh...so you know how much everyone spent on you.

BIG DADDY: Heh, heh, yeah, that's sensible. I like you, son. *(Opens envelope)* Magnolia Farms Country Club.

(Everyone reacts with ooohs and ahhhs.)

BIG DADDY: Lifetime membership!

(This time only AMANDA reacts happily. Everyone else catches on.)

STANLEY: Hey, Big Amanda. Ain't it 'bout time for the birthday cake? I'll make room. *(Goes to grab papers)*

BIG DADDY: I don't want any cake. I just want to open the rest of my crap. *(Picks up papers)* Who's this one from? There's no card.

STANLEY: *(Grabs it)* That's from Blanche and me. But I don't think it'll fit. I'll exchange it and get you a new present.

BIG DADDY: Big Amanda can take care of that tomorrow. Hand it over, boy.

MAGGIE: Why Stanley, that package looks awfully familiar.

STANLEY: It looks like a package. They all look alike.

MAGGIE: I remember now! I wrapped that one myself as a favor to sister Blanche. It's a lovely gift. I think Big Daddy will be so pleased.

STANLEY: You must be mistaken, Maggie the Cat.

MAGGIE: Well, then let's have Big Daddy open it up, so I can see.

STANLEY: Shut up, Maggie.

MAGGIE: Open the present, Big Daddy. We all want to see what Stanley got for you.

BIG DADDY: Give it to me, Stanley. It couldn't be any worse than the Spirograph. Give it here! *(Takes it)*

(MAGGIE moves around behind BIG DADDY and peers over his shoulder.)

BIG DADDY: Why, what in the devil...

BLANCHE: It looks like pages out of an old, old book. Perhaps *The Canterbury Tales* or a letter from Robert Browning.

MAGGIE: Why, it's papers signed by a doctor of repute claiming Blanche to be certifiably insane!

BIG DADDY: Hardly seems like a fittin' birthday present.

AMANDA: My baby, my beautiful baby! Wigged out! Oh, the shame!

BLANCHE: Well, I am appalled. I will not stand here and be smeared with such vile accusations, when it was I who led the French troops forward into Baton Rouge without so much as a Red Cross doughnut to bolster my continence...I mean my constitution... Why are you all looking at me?... I'm just a fright.... You'll make me crazy with your glaring. Don't look at me! *(Runs into bathroom)*

MITCH: Blanche! *(Runs after her and stands at bathroom door)*

AMANDA: Oh my baby, my poor baby!

MAGGIE: *(To STANLEY)* Why you no-scruples monster! Giving Big Daddy sworn papers by a distinguished physician of a prestigious hospital proving poor

Blanche legally crazy so you could take advantage of his sympathetic nature and swindle your Big Daddy-in-law out of all his money. Well, Big Daddy is smarter than that. You won't get one penny.

STANLEY: That's a lie.

AMANDA: No, I doubt I'll get your money back without a receipt. Maybe I could exchange it for some socks. Would you like some nice socks, Big Daddy?

BIG DADDY: This comes as quite a shock. I think I'll go downstairs and think a spell.

(*He starts for the door.* AMANDA *grabs on to his waist and starts the conga line back out.* MAGGIE *grabs* BRICK *and jumps on the back of the line. As* AMANDA *exits we hear...*)

LAURA: (*Off*) Look, Big Daddy, I made it up the stairs all by myself.

AMANDA: (*Off*) Grab onto the back of the line, Laura.

(STANLEY *is left alone onstage. The lights dim. [A soft red spot comes up on him.] He drops to his knees and pulls at his hair in anguish.* MAGGIE *appears in the doorway.*)

MAGGIE: You can kneel all you want, brother-man, but you don't have a prayer.

STANLEY: If it isn't Maggie the Cat come back to bury her shit.

MAGGIE: I came to make sure you didn't steal anything else out of my suitcase. You deserved what you got, pawing through my personal belongings like a mongrel dog sniffin' for a bone.

STANLEY: Put away your claws, Maggie. I ain't your scratchin' post, and I ain't your bird perch of a husband. When I get scratched I scratch back.

MAGGIE: (*Moving closer*) That sounds remotely like a threat.

STANLEY: There ain't nothin' remote about it. (*Grabs her by the shoulders*) I could kill you with my bare hands.

MAGGIE: There's no need for that. You could kill me with your breath.

STANLEY: You're not a cat, you're a leopard.

MAGGIE: My skin's a little blotchy from the heat...

STANLEY: No, you're wild. Too wild for your own good. Sooner or later you come across the king of the jungle and pick a fight you cannot win.

MAGGIE: I think I followed better when we were having the chicken bone argument.

STANLEY: It's time you were housebroken, Maggie.

MAGGIE: What, are you going to spread some papers out on the floor?

STANLEY: (*Dragging her over to the table, he grabs the papers and flings them across the bed as the music wells up.*) No, not on the floor, Maggie. Never on the floor. (*He slowly pushes her onto the bed.*)

(*A spotlight on* BLANCHE *as she emerges from behind the curtain and sees them.*)

BLANCHE: Is this a party game? Are we playing post office?

(*Lights fade to black on* STANLEY *and* MAGGIE.)

BLANCHE: Who has a special delivery for me? First class only...no solicitors please...

(*Spot fades to black on* BLANCHE.)

Scene Two

(All of the family except AMANDA *and* STANLEY *are onstage.* MITCH *is consoling Blanche.* BIG DADDY *sits at the table making Spirograph designs.* LAURA *is playing with her animals.* MAGGIE *and* BRICK *are at the other side of the table from* BIG DADDY.*)*

MAGGIE: *(Taking a drink out of* BRICK's *hand)* Don't you think you've had enough of that, Baby? I don't know what's gotten into you. You look at me so strangely this morning, as if you're lookin' right through me.

BIG DADDY: That boy's been liftin' his glass too often and too early. Ain't proper to have a drink before ten a.m. Is he becoming an alcoholic? I can't tolerate alcoholics.

MAGGIE: Oh no, Big Daddy. Brick is just drinkin' because it soothes his sore throat.

BIG DADDY: A good slug of 10W40 will take care of that throat.

MAGGIE: Also he's a little upset about Blanche having to be locked up and all.

MITCH: Who are you trying to kid, Maggie? Brick doesn't give a damn about Blanche. He drinks because he feels sorry for himself. He hasn't developed the taste for blood the rest of you have...

BLANCHE: Dracula was here last night. He was bending over Maggie in her bed.

MITCH: Blanche, I value your opinion as a person, but there is a time for holding your tongue...

*(*BLANCHE *grabs her tongue.* MITCH *pulls her hand away.)*

MITCH: ...and I think you should be quiet and rest for now.

BLANCHE: I shall string some garlic. We can hang it on the Christmas tree.

MITCH: Good idea, my sweet.

(BLANCHE *exits.*)

MITCH: Where was I?

MAGGIE: I believe you were calling us all bloodthirsty vampires, Mr O'Connor.

MITCH: That's right. See, Brick never developed that cruel streak to protect himself. So he turns his anger inward. To punish himself for being a failure...a failure as a man. That's why Brick drinks.

MAGGIE: Brick, a failure? Don't make me laugh. Who are you to judge the quality of a man, when your mama still lays out your clothes and gives you a Mr Bubble bath every Saturday night.

MITCH: Leave my mother out of this.

MAGGIE: Cuts your meat, blows on your soup, draws little hearts on your peanut butter sandwiches.

BIG DADDY: Enough! Leave the sissy alone! Maggie, you're as feisty as a mare in a glue factory. Didn't you get enough sleep last night?

MAGGIE: (*Rubbing* BRICK's *neck*) No, I can't say as I did get very much sleep last night, Big Daddy.

BIG DADDY: Ho, ho! Ain't that the same slip you was wearing last night, daughter-in-law?

MAGGIE: Why so it is.

BIG DADDY: Ho, ho, ho!

(BLANCHE *enters.*)

BLANCHE: Is Santy Claus here?

(BIG DADDY *turns away.*)

BLANCHE: Where is my candy cane? *(Sits on* BRICK'*s lap)* I want a dolly, a pretty little dolly that looks like that lady...*(Points to* MAGGIE*)*...and a bottle of battery acid.

MAGGIE: *(Yanks* BLANCHE *up)* Get off my husband, you lunatic.

BLANCHE: Thank you, Little Elf.

MITCH: Come to me, my darling.

BLANCHE: Heathcliff, is that really you?

BIG DADDY: Mitch, come over here.

(MITCH *slides* BLANCHE *down the wall so she is seated on the floor. She starts singing, "Where is Thumbkin?")*

BIG DADDY: She seems to be getting worse.

MITCH: You think so?

BIG DADDY: *(nods)* Well, it won't be long now. When are the... *(Looks at* BLANCHE*)* delivery men expected.

(MITCH *is puzzled.*)

BIG DADDY: The dogcatchers...when are they coming?

(MITCH *is perplexed.*)

BIG DADDY: When are the meathandlers coming to haul Blanche to the funny farm?!

(BLANCHE *screams, crawls a little bit upstage against the bathroom door, and begins to suck her thumb.*)

MITCH: It's all right, Blanche. Big Daddy's only making a joke. *(To* BIG DADDY*)* Any time now.

BIG DADDY: Look at her. My eldest child. My namesake.

MITCH: Your name is Blanche?

BIG DADDY: Why do you think everyone calls me Big Daddy? She was such a beauty. I can't bear to see her like this. Go throw your coat over her, Mitch.

(MITCH *goes over to* BLANCHE, *throws his suit jacket over her head and sits embracing her.* STANLEY *enters from bathroom, stepping over* BLANCHE *as she falls backwards.*)

STANLEY: Good morning, Big Daddy, Mitch. Good morning, Maggie. (*Grabs* MAGGIE, *bends her over backwards and kisses her neck*) So did I miss anything? (*Goes over to cooler*) Excuse me kid. (*He digs down to the bottom and takes a beer out and puts an ice cube in his mouth.*)

LAURA: Where's my giraffe?

(STANLEY *pauses, then turns and spits ice cube across room into cooler.*)

MITCH: The hospital is sending over two attendants to pick up Blanche.

STANLEY: Oh, that's too bad.

LAURA: Big Daddy, Stanley upset my glass animals.

BIG DADDY: Hush up, child, I've heard enough out of you. (*To* STANLEY) Is that all you can say about your own wife bein' dragged off to the nuthouse?

(BLANCHE *screams again from under the jacket.*)

MITCH: She doesn't like that word.

BIG DADDY: She don't like the word fart either.

(BLANCHE *lets out a muffled scream.*)

BIG DADDY: But however sweet you say it, a fart is still a fart, and a nuthouse is still a nuthouse. Now, Stanley, do you or don't you love my daughter Blanche?

STANLEY: Is this a trick question?

BIG DADDY: Answer me!

STANLEY: I love her as much as the day I married her.

LAURA: Now you mustn't pay any attention to Stanley. He can't help being a pig. Oh, I'm sorry, Porky. I didn't mean to hurt your feelings.

BIG DADDY: Laura, what the hell are you up to over there?

LAURA: I'm trying to calm my animals down. Stanley upset them terribly, and they're perspiring with fear.

BIG DADDY: Child, get over here. It's time you and I had a little talk.

LAURA: Oh, Mama and I already had that talk. I threw up four times.

BIG DADDY: Not that talk. It's about your collection.

LAURA: If it's about your birthday present, don't worry. The other animals will miss him at first but they'll get over it.

BIG DADDY: Yes, my birthday present. Let me show you something, Laura. (Gets box from table) Do you know what this is?

LAURA: It's your birthday present.

BIG DADDY: Do you know what's inside?

LAURA: My glass unicorn.

(BIG DADDY opens the box and pours out the water. LAURA kneels at the puddle.)

LAURA: My unicorn!

BIG DADDY: It's not a unicorn. It's a puddle. You've been living a lie, child. And if there's one thing I hate more than getting an ice cube for my birthday, it's mendacity. You're a woman now, Laura. It's time you started actin' like one. Have Maggie lend you a slip, go out and find yourself a husband and start a family you don't have to keep in a cooler.

LAURA: Yes, I understand. I hate you, but I understand.

BIG DADDY: Nothing would make me happier than to have a grandson to carry on the family name. Perhaps to live in this house, which my granddaddy built, when I'm gone.

MAGGIE: I have an announcement to make. I am with child.

(BRICK *faints.*)

STANLEY: How can that be? It was just last night.

BIG DADDY: You were listenin'. Shame on you, boy.

STANLEY: Listenin'? I was there.

BIG DADDY: Spyin'! You cad! We have a name for boys like you where I come from.

STANLEY: Yeah. Active participant.

MAGGIE: Stanley, can I have a word with you privately?

BIG DADDY: Hold on! Boy, are you sayin' you entered Maggie's bed last night?

STANLEY: I entered more than her bed.

MAGGIE: That's a lie! Don't believe it, Brick.

STANLEY: That baby is the fruit of my hocks.

MITCH: Loins.

STANLEY: Loins.

(BLANCHE *screams and throws the coat off her head.*)

BLANCHE: (*Getting up*) There's rosemary. That's for remembrance. And there is pansies. That's for thought. Oh how the whale becomes it. It is the false sewer that stole his master's daughter. And will he not come

again? And will he not come again? (*To* MITCH)
Give me your cigarette case, I'm stuck.

BIG DADDY: (*To* MAGGIE) And will he not come again?!
What is Blanche talking about, Maggie?

MAGGIE: Hamlet, I think, but I don't know where the
whale comes in. Maybe that's supposed to be you.

BIG DADDY: Dracula came to Maggie's bed. What did
Blanche mean by that?! What did she see? Tell me the
truth, Maggie the Cat!

MAGGIE: We were rehearsing a play?

BIG DADDY: Mendacity! I'm surrounded by lies and
deceit and mendacity!

MITCH: And redundancy.

BIG DADDY: Well, I have tolerated as much as I'm going
to tolerate. This whole family crawls around like insects
in a web of deceit and greed and weird behavioral
traits. Mendacity! Laura lives in a world of illusion.
Blanche has been living in the past and boasting of
a virtue that hasn't been in existence since the docks
opened up. Stanley crawling into Maggie's bed.
Maggie, telling me you're pregnant hoping to play on
an old man's generosity. Lust, greed, and mendacity!
Brick, my only son, lives in a cloud of whiskey-wrought
mendacity, trying to live up to our expectations of him.
When we all know he'll never amount to anything.
For crying out loud, he's just a mannequin. It's all
mendacity! Well, no more. I am ashamed of every one
of you. I'm repulsed by your greed and your lies. Look
at you all standing there dripping in your own slime.
I will not have it in my house! From now on the truth
will be told! What have you worms got to say for
yourselves?!

MITCH, BLANCHE, STANLEY, MAGGIE: You're dyin'!

BIG DADDY: There's something to be said for mendacity.

MITCH: We only lied to spare you the worry, sir. After all, it was your birthday.

BIG DADDY: I don't need your coddling, do you hear?! Somebody fix me a whiskey.

(MITCH *goes to bar.*)

BIG DADDY: So this is how it's to be, huh? Well, if I'm going to face Death, I'll meet him on my terms, I'll play chess with the sonofabitch. Hell, it's my house, we'll play horseshoes! I ain't givin' up without a fight.

MAGGIE: That's the spirit, Big Daddy.

BIG DADDY: Oh, shut up. Can't you see I'm dying! *(Pause)* Mitch, how much longer?

MITCH: A few days, a few months, it's hard to say.

BIG DADDY: I mean for the whiskey. Hurry it up, boy.

(MITCH *takes whiskey to* BIG DADDY, *who drinks it down.*)

BIG DADDY: Ahh! I'll miss that. In fact, I miss it already. Mitch!

(MITCH *pours him another.*)

BIG DADDY: Things seem so clear now. Staring Death in the sockets makes a man reevaluate things. *(Deep breath)* Smell the room. *(They all do.)* It smells of life! Of fresh cut grass, and fine, old cigars. Of rug shampoo, and *(Deep sniff)*, the absence of that stench called Mendacity. I'm going to go scare up a game of softball with the domestics.

MAGGIE: Big Daddy, this may sound heartless and cruel right now, but Stanley wants to know who gets the house after you pass.

STANLEY: I do not!

MAGGIE: Of course you don't, but somebody's got to end up with it.

BIG DADDY: Gather round the table. *(He puts the deed on the table.)* There it is. The deed to the whole kit 'n' caboodle. You know, all that's left of a man when he dies is what he has nurtured on this earth: his family and his land. Lucky for you I still care about my land. I, Big Daddy, hereby bequeath the estate, lands, buildings, slaves—

MITCH: Field hands.

BIG DADDY: Field hands..., water rights, light fixtures, blah-blah-blah, herein called Belle Reve...unto my only son, Brick DuBois.

(A stunned silence, in which MAGGIE jubilantly leaps about upstage of the others, like a World Series winner.)

BIG DADDY: *(To BRICK)* You're the hope of this family, Brick. Don't screw it up. *(Holding out pen)* Sign it, son. *(Pause)* You hear me, Brick-Boy, sign the deed. *(Pause)* Don't mock me boy, take the pen!

MAGGIE: *(Stops celebrating and rushes to BRICK)* Brick, what's the trouble, baby?

BIG DADDY: The insolent, ungrateful—!

MAGGIE: No, Big Daddy, it's just a writer's block. Come on, Brick.

BIG DADDY: What did I ever do to you to deserve this? What did I ever do?... Now, you're not still mad about that?

MAGGIE: Give me the pen. I'll guide his hand.

STANLEY: He ain't signing. It's as plain as my clothes. He's out, Big Daddy.

BIG DADDY: Yes, Brick's out! It all goes to Blanche then, all of it!

MAGGIE: No!

STANLEY: *(Rushes to the zoned-out* BLANCHE*)* Ya hear that, Blanche? Ya hear that?! *(Pause)* Stomp twice if ya hear that.

*(*BLANCHE *stomps twice.)*

STANLEY: It's ours, Blanche! And yours too, I promise. Remember...the Napoleonic Code.

BLANCHE: *(Her eyes gloss over and her back straightens.)* Yes, of course, Mr Bonaparte. Where do I sign?

STANLEY: Right here, Blanche.

(As BLANCHE *goes to the table, takes pen, and signs, a bizarre echo chorus is heard. Voices from her past.)*

ECHO VOICES: You are Blanche Kowalski now...She was quite the flower...DuBois means White Woods...Get off my husband, you lunatic!...Napoleonic Code...My beautiful baby, wigged out!...Napoleonic Code... Blanche, are you unwell?...Napoleonic Code-leonic-code-leonic-code-leonic-coooo... *(*VOICES *cut to silence.)*

STANLEY: Done!

BIG DADDY: *(Looking at deed)* Marie Antoinette? She signed it Marie Antoinette.

BLANCHE: Oui, oui, Louis!

STANLEY: Blanche, don't be yankin' Big Daddy around now. Sign it right. It needs your John Hancock....No, no! That's a figure of speech. Write B...L...

MAGGIE: Time's up.

STANLEY: Come on, give her a break! At least she wrote something! At least she's got motor skills!

MAGGIE: Her time is up, Stanley.

BIG DADDY: All of your time is up! All of ya! My legacy to this earth is a French monarch and a mannequin! Oh, my guts hurt. Laura? Where's Laura?

LAURA: Here, Big Daddy.

BIG DADDY: Come here, Laura-Child. It's yours. The whole estate is yours.

MAGGIE: Come now, Big Daddy, what does Laura know about farming? The animal sounds on a See & Say?

BIG DADDY: Hush up, woman.

MAGGIE: But Big Daddy—!

STANLEY: The man said hush up, Maggie. *(He takes* MAGGIE *forcefully by the arm to the bar, away from the others.)*

LAURA: You're giving Belle Reve to me? But...I don't know the first thing about property.

BIG DADDY: Can you write your name?

LAURA: Yes.

BIG DADDY: In this family, that makes you a qualified home owner. Sign here.

LAURA: I'm not very good at cursive.

STANLEY: Think about it, Maggie. Laura wins the ranch. So what?! With Big Daddy out of the way and Laura being so stupid, how long before she needs a guardian for her estate. A legal guardian, if you snatch my thrust.

MAGGIE: *(Snatching his thrust)* Why Stanley, an actual idea coming out of your head. I'm impressed. Pour me a drink.

STANLEY: You may find that this no-neck Neanderthal brute of a pig isn't half bad company for you, Maggie the Cat.

MAGGIE: *(Watching* LAURA*)* And you may find, Stanley the Talking Mule, that Laura has already found her legal guardian.

LAURA: Before I sign it...Mitch...

(MITCH *goes to her.)*

LAURA: ...I just want to say thank you for being so nice. You were right about...what you said before, about... about the truck hitting me and my teeth and nails... I can't recall the whole metaphor, but you were right! I have to stop running away from life. *(Smiles)* You're the kindest man I ever met.

(They kiss. A Pause)

LAURA: I don't want a large wedding....

(MITCH *spits/wipes off kiss.)*

LAURA: ...we'll have it right here at Belle Reve. Big Daddy and I will be wheeled down the aisle side by side, and Maggie and Blanche will be the matrons of honor, and Mama will place jonquils all about, and Stanley—

MITCH: Laura—

LAURA: Stanley will park cars—

MITCH: Laura—

LAURA: And at the reception, Tony Orlando will call me up to the stage—

MITCH: Laura, stop it, please. There is no wedding for us. I don't love you. What we had yesterday was... it was just a... *(Suddenly)* You could really get Tony Orlando?

LAURA: You don't love me?

MITCH: I like you, Laura. But I love another. I love Blanche.

LAURA: Blanche!

MITCH: I'm sorry. I shouldn't have encouraged you. But someday you'll find a man—

LAURA: I don't want a man, I want you!

MITCH: You can't live in a dream world, Laura, but you can't live at my place either.

LAURA: Then I don't want to live anywhere! I don't want Belle Reve! I don't want anything! I just want to vomit! *(Runs into bathroom and slams the door behind her)*

MAGGIE: Laura, baby! Laura!

STANLEY: Come on out and sign the papers, sweetheart.

BIG DADDY: Leave her be. Laura's the only honest child I got. She looks around, sees this family, and throws up. Well, I didn't help my granddaddy build Belle Reve from the stony ground with my bare hands only to have my own kin spite me in my last days. Louisiana law says I can't take it with me? Well maybe I shall! *(Pulls out his watch)* Here, Brick, here's your watch. Can you hear it ticking, ticking down what's left of Big Daddy? It's gears are snapping and popping away my life...but if you listen carefully, it's ticking down to the end of the whole DuBois family. Listen. *(Rhythmically)* Tough, tit, tough, tit, tough, tit, tough, tit, you, don't, get, the, house, you, gree, dee, pare, a, sites, ha, ha, ha, ha,..... You hear it, Maggie the Cat? *(Pushes watch in MAGGIE's face)* Stanley? *(The same to STANLEY)* Whoever you are. *(Pushes watch at MITCH)* Can you hear it ticking away?! *(Gives watch to BRICK)* Here, you can keep the watch. I'm taking with me something much more valuable. I, Big Daddy, hereby bequeath the estate to...Big Daddy, you cheating sacks of dookie! *(Starts to eat the deed)*

MAGGIE: Big Daddy, don't be a fool!

BIG DADDY: *(Chewing)* Mmmmm. Fine property.

MITCH: Please, Big Daddy!

STANLEY: Leave him be. Leave Big Daddy be. If this is his choice, we should respect it. *(To* BIG DADDY*)* I hope you choke.

AMANDA: *(Entering)* Blanche, dear, it's time...there's... two bandoliers with autoharps request your company in their milk truck downstairs.

BLANCHE: They've been expected. But I must bid my farewells. *(To* BIG DADDY*)* My dear Shep Huntleigh, your poem was beautiful. Yes, yes, destroy it now before the Russians catch us! *(To* MAGGIE*)* Why Margaret, what a fetching slip.

MAGGIE: This is my party slip. My fetching slip is at home.

BLANCHE: I was mistaken. *(To* STANLEY*)* Stanley, I shall be downstairs with Louis Pasteur and his orchestra. Do join us for lawn darts.

STANLEY: Yeah. Later.

AMANDA: Blanche, dear...

BLANCHE: One moment, coachman. *(To* MITCH*)* Mr Bonaparte, if you will be traveling with me today you must get your big hat. The carriage awaits.

MITCH: I...I'm staying, Blanche. There's nothing I can do for you where you're going. Besides, there's the deed. It'll be a day or so before I can go through the paperwork. Will you be all right?

BLANCHE: Yes, I believe I shall. But before I depart, it would mean a great deal if you could all, one last time, kneel to me as your queen.

STANLEY: Blanche!

BIG DADDY: This is my house, you hear! Kneel to the queen.

(*All kneel to* BLANCHE.)

BLANCHE: I have always depended upon the quality of strangeness.

(BLANCHE *exits.* MITCH *watches her go from the window.*)

AMANDA: (*Rushing to* BIG DADDY, *embracing him*) Oh, Big Daddy!

BIG DADDY: Be strong, Big Amanda, be strong...there, there now, it's all right, all right, okay, that's enough...leggo! Never did get my cake.

AMANDA: Well, I set aside a slice just for you. (*Gets the cake*) Here it is, with a candle in it. Let's have a wish shall we? (*She begins to light the candle, while across the room...*)

MAGGIE: Missing Blanche?

STANLEY: I will for a while... (*Pause*)

MAGGIE: Done?

STANLEY: Yup.

MAGGIE: (*Grabbing* STANLEY *by the T-shirt and pulling him down*) You're callous and shallow and beastly and—

STANLEY: Stop!... Never on the floor.

(*They flop onto the bed.* MITCH *has lit a cigarette for himself and* BRICK. MITCH *moves to fire escape as* BLANCHE's *face appears against the window glass, as if she has climbed the house.* MAGGIE *and* STANLEY *are busy on the bed.*)

BIG DADDY: (*To* AMANDA) Big Amanda, I've been afforded the chance to see the lies and deceit stripped away from my life, and, after seeing the true makings of this family, I'm glad I'm dying.

AMANDA: Dying? Are you dying?

BIG DADDY: Oh, shut up.

AMANDA: Doctor Adams said it was— You're dying?!

BIG DADDY: Shut up, woman.

AMANDA: Dying? Really?!

BIG DADDY: I mean it, woman!

(*Lights on* BIG DADDY *and* AMANDA *fade out as the song* "Seasons in the Sun" *begins to play...*STANLEY *and* MAGGIE *roll over and light cigarettes...*BLANCHE *remains in the window.*)

BIG DADDY: Goodbye to you, it's hard to die,
When all the birds are singing in the sky,
...Etc.

MITCH: (*On fire escape*) I didn't stay to go through Big Daddy's paperwork. I didn't even stay for cake. I left that house as quick as a wink, took the transfer named Desire and got the elevated out of there. I have since traveled a great deal, unable to settle into a family for fear of what it might become. For the memory of the DuBois family pursues me, attacking me unawares on dark streets, beating me up and taking my money. Sometimes it is the glimpse of a pocket watch, or a cotton slip in a store window...or the mannequin that wears it. The strains of Helen Reddy in a dentist's office, or an ice cube silently dying, left too long in the sun.

We are not meant to be stripped of our dreams and fantasies. Our mendacities, if you will. We are meant to hope, to wish on candles, and to wait for the men in the ice cream truck. Alas, I am more faithful to them than I intended to be. I bought an autoharp. Blow out your candles, Big Daddy...

(BIG DADDY *wets his fingers and presses out the flame.*)

MITCH: ...and so goodbye.

BIG DADDY: *(In darkness)* Aagghh! Goddammit! That hurts like hell!

END OF PLAY

PROPERTY LIST

Several well-worn suitcases
Cigarettes and matches
Cooler containing ice cubes and beer bottles
Record player with old 45 records
Cardboard record with picture of Bobby Sherman
Several bottles or decanters of whisky, with glasses
High school yearbook
High school theater program
Playing cards and poker chips
Bags of pretzels and cheese balls
Silver cigarette case
Pocket watch
Gift-wrapped presents:
  Spirograph set
  Country club membership card
  Cartoon calendar
  Empty box containing melted ice cube
Papers:
  BLANCHE's commitment papers
  LAURA's business school letter
  BIG DADDY's will on edible rice paper

BROADWAY PLAY PUBLISHING INC

ONE ACT COLLECTIONS

THE COLORED MUSEUM

ENSEMBLE STUDIO THEATER MARATHON `84

FACING FORWARD

GIANTS HAVE US IN THEIR BOOKS

ONE ACTS AND MONOLOGUES FOR WOMEN

ORCHARDS

ORGASMO ADULTO ESCAPES FROM THE ZOO

PLAYS BY LOUIS PHILLIPS

ROOTS IN WATER

SHORT PIECES FROM THE NEW DRAMATISTS

WHAT A MAN WEIGHS &
THE WORLD AT ABSOLUTE ZERO

BROADWAY PLAY PUBLISHING INC

PLAYS WITH MORE WOMEN THAN MEN

BESIDE HERSELF

A BRIGHT ROOM CALLED DAY

CHURCH OF THE HOLY GHOST

DAME LORRAINE

A DARING BRIDE

GOONA GOONA

THE LADIES OF FISHER COVE

MINK SONATA

ONLY IN AMERICA

ON THE VERGE

PECONG

PHANTASIE

RAIN. SOME FISH. NO ELEPHANTS.

SHOW AND TELL

STARSTRUCK

STONEWALL JACKSON'S HOUSE

UNFINISHED WOMEN CRY IN A NO MAN'S LAND WHILE
A BIRD DIES IN A GILDED CAGE

WHAT A MAN WEIGHS

BROADWAY PLAY PUBLISHING INC

TOP TEN BEST SELLING FULL-LENGTH PLAYS AND FULL-LENGTH PLAY COLLECTIONS

BATTERY

THE IMMIGRANT

NATIVE SPEECH

ONE FLEA SPARE

ON THE VERGE

PLAYS BY TONY KUSHNER
(CONTAINING A BRIGHT ROOM CALLED DAY,
THE ILLUSION, & SLAVS!)

PRELUDE TO A KISS

THE PROMISE

TALES OF THE LOST FORMICANS

TO GILLIAN ON HER 37TH BIRTHDAY